A Technique
for Producing Ideas

by James Webb Young

IBC パブリッシング

A Technique for Producing Ideas by James Webb Young

Copyright© 2003 by The McGraw-Hill Companies, Inc.

English reprint rights arranged with The McGraw-Hill Companies through Japan UNI Agency, Inc., Tokyo.

はじめに

　ラダーシリーズは、「はしご（ladder）」を使って一歩一歩上を目指すように、学習者の実力に合わせ、無理なくステップアップできるよう開発された英文リーダーのシリーズです。

　リーディング力をつけるためには、繰り返したくさん読むこと、いわゆる「多読」がもっとも効果的な学習法であると言われています。多読では、「1. 速く 2. 訳さず英語のまま 3. なるべく辞書を使わず」に読むことが大切です。スピードを計るなど、速く読むよう心がけましょう（たとえば TOEIC® テストの音声スピードはおよそ 1 分間に 150 語です）。そして一語ずつ訳すのではなく、英語を英語のまま理解するくせをつけるようにします。こうして読み続けるうちに語感がついてきて、だんだんと英語が理解できるようになるのです。まずは、ラダーシリーズの中からあなたのレベルに合った本を選び、少しずつ英文に慣れ親しんでください。たくさんの本を手にとるうちに、英文書がすらすら読めるようになってくるはずです。

《本シリーズの特徴》
- 中学校レベルから中級者レベルまで5段階に分かれています。自分に合ったレベルからスタートしてください。
- クラシックから現代文学、ノンフィクション、ビジネスと幅広いジャンルを扱っています。あなたの興味に合わせてタイトルを選べます。
- 巻末のワードリストで、いつでもどこでも単語の意味を確認できます。レベル1、2では、文中の全ての単語が、レベル3以上は中学校レベル外の単語が掲載されています。
- カバーにヘッドホーンマークのついているタイトルは、オーディオ・サポートがあります。ウェブから購入／ダウンロードし、リスニング教材としても併用できます。

《使用語彙について》
レベル1：中学校で学習する単語約1000語
レベル2：レベル1の単語＋使用頻度の高い単語約300語
レベル3：レベル1の単語＋使用頻度の高い単語約600語
レベル4：レベル1の単語＋使用頻度の高い単語約1000語
レベル5：語彙制限なし

Contents

Foreword by Keith Reinhard.. vii
Foreword by William Bernbach xi
Prefatory Note xv

How It Started 1
The Formula of Experience 4
The Pareto Theory 7
Training the Mind 11
Combining Old Elements 13
Ideas Are New Combinations 17
The Mental Digestive Process 26
"Constantly Thinking About It" 31
The Final Stage 34
Some After-Thoughts 37

Word List 44

読みはじめる前に

●本書に登場する学者、作家

Pareto ヴィルフレード・パレート（Vilfredo Pareto, 1848-1923）　イタリアの経済学者、社会学者。全体の2割の高額所得者の所得が、国全体の所得の約8割を占めるという「パレートの法則」を提唱。

Dr. Harold Lasswell ハロルド・ラスウェル博士（Harold Dwight Lasswell, 1902-1978）　アメリカを代表する政治学者。現代政治学の名著『権力と人間』『政治―動態分析』を著す。プロパガンダを「シンボルの操作により、人間の行動に影響を与えるテクニック」とした。

Veblen ソースティン・ヴェブレン（Thorstein Bunde Veblen, 1857-1929）　アメリカの経済学者。*Theory of the Leisure Class*『有閑階級の理論』を著した。

Riesman デイヴィッド・リースマン（David Riesman, 1909-2002）　アメリカの社会学者。*The Lonely Crowd*『孤独な群衆』を著した。

Maupassant モーパッサン（Guy de Maupassant, 1850-1893）　19世紀フランス文学を代表する小説家、劇作家、詩人。おなじくフランスの作家フロベールを師として、『脂肪の塊』『女の一生』などの名作を生み出した。

Jane Austen ジェーン・オースティン（Jane Austen, 1775-1817）　平凡な出来事をユーモラスかつ鋭く描いたイギリスの女流作家。『高慢と偏見』はイギリス文学を代表する作品。

Hayakawa S.I.ハヤカワ（Samuel. I. Hayakawa, 1906-1992）　日系アメリカ人の言語学者。*Language in Thought and Action*『思考と行動における言語』を著した。

Foreword

*By Keith Reinhard, Chairman,
DDB Worldwide*

How can a book first published in the 1940s be important to creative people on today's cutting edge? By answering the question that inspired James Webb Young to write this remarkable little volume in the first place: "How do you get ideas?" The blank page or screen that awaits a transforming idea today is just as intimidating as ever. Maybe more so, because our advanced environments demand even better ideas and more of them. The steps laid down by Young are the surest path to that incomparable thrill of discovery the author describes as the "Eureka! I have it!" stage.

When I first encountered this book, I was still a working creative director. I had never heard of James Webb Young but, like most other creative people in advertising, I was a fan and follower of Bill Bernbach, who revolutionized the ad world in the late fifties and sixties with his rule-breaking work for a number of brands, most notably the Volkswagen Beetle. When I saw that Bill had written a foreword to the book, I knew I should check it out.

What I found was the most concise and illuminating description of the creative process I had ever read. I sent out at once for enough copies to supply the entire creative department, and since then, I've handed out hundreds more.

For creative people just getting started, Young offers both guidance and the assurance that coming up with an idea is a process, not an accident. For those more experienced, Young comforts us with the knowledge that what we might have thought was pure intuition is actually a series of steps that can be described and taught and repeated over and over again. And, should this little book fall into the hands of those who say "I've never had an idea in my life," they just might surprise themselves.

Foreword

*By William Bernbach, Chairman,
Worldwide and Chief Executive Officer,
Doyle Dane Bernbach Inc.*

James Webb Young conveys in his little book something more valuable than the most learned and detailed texts on the subject of advertising. For he is talking about the soul of a piece of communications and not merely the flesh and bones. He is talking about the idea. A chemist can inexpensively put together a human body. What he can't do is spark it with life. Mr. Young writes about the creative spark, the ideas, which bring spirit and life to an advertisement. Nothing is more important to the practice of our craft.

Mr. Young is in the tradition of some of our greatest thinkers when he describes the workings of the creative process. It is a tribute to him that such scientific giants as Bertrand Russell and Albert Einstein have written similarly on this subject. They agree that knowledge is basic to good creative thinking but that it is not enough, that this knowledge must be digested and eventually emerge in the form of fresh, new combinations and relationships. Einstein refers to this as intuition, which he considers the only path to new insights.

The quality of the ideas you get cannot be guaranteed, and James Webb Young would, I am sure, be the first one to tell you this. That quality would be the result of all the forces in your life that have played on you, including your genes. But you will be making the most of those forces and all your natural equipment if you follow the procedures he outlines so simply and lucidly.

We are indebted to Mr. Young for getting to

the heart of the matter. The result of many years of work in advertising have proved to him that the key element in communications success is the production of relevant and dramatic ideas. He not only makes this point vividly for us but shows us the road to that goal.

Prefatory Note

These thoughts were first presented to graduate students in advertising at the School of Business of the University of Chicago and later before several gatherings of active advertising practitioners. This accounts for the informal tone.

The subject is properly one which belongs to the professional psychologist, which I am not. This treatment of it, therefore, can have value only as an expression of the personal experience of one who has had to earn his living by producing what were alleged to be ideas.

It was first prepared one Sunday afternoon when I had to consider what I should say to a

Monday class. No literature on the subject was at the moment available; nor had I any recollection of having seen any. Since then many readers of this book have called my attention to writings on the same subject, from different areas of experience; and there have been published several recent books with something worthwhile to say on this topic. On the last page of this edition I have listed three which I have found stimulating.

James Webb Young
Rancho de la Cañada,
Peña Blanca, New Mexico
July 1960

How It Started

One day in my last year as an advertising agency executive in Chicago I had a telephone call from the western advertising manager of a well-known magazine.

He asked if he could see me immediately on a matter of importance. Shortly thereafter he arrived in my office, somewhat out of breath.

"We are having a meeting today," he said, "of our entire western sales staff. Its purpose is to discuss how we can improve our selling.

"In our discussions we have tried to analyze the selling methods of other successful publications and salesmen. And among these we have been particularly impressed by the success of Mr. Kobler in his selling of the American Weekly.

"After studying just why he is so successful we have come to the conclusion that it all rests on just one thing: he doesn't sell space; he sells Ideas.

"And so," he continued, with enthusiasm, "we have decided that that is just what we are going to do. From here on we are not going to sell space at all. Beginning tomorrow morning every single one of us is going to sell *Ideas*!"

I said I thought that was just dandy but wondered what it was that he wanted to discuss with me.

"Well," he said, somewhat ruefully, "we could see that what we ought to do is to sell ideas, all right. But after that we sort of got stuck.

"What we are not clear about is just how to get ideas.

"So I said maybe you could tell us, and that is what I am here for.

How It Started

"You have produced a lot of advertising ideas. Just how do you get them? The boys are waiting for me to come back and tell them."

Now I know that if I had not been so flattered by this question, and if my questioner had not been so obviously serious in asking it, I would have had a hearty fit of laughing at this point.

I thought at the time that I had never heard a funnier or more naive question. And I was completely unable to give any helpful answer to it.

But it struck me afterward that maybe the question "How do you get ideas?" wasn't as silly as it sounded. Maybe there was some answer to it. And off and on I thought about it.

The Formula of Experience

An idea, I thought, has some of that mysterious quality which romance lends to tales of the sudden appearance of islands in the South Seas.

There, according to ancient mariners, in spots where the charts showed only deep blue sea, there would suddenly appear a lovely atoll above the surface of the waters. An air of magic hung about it.

And so it is, I thought, with Ideas. They appear just as suddenly above the surface of the mind—and with that same air of magic and unaccountability.

But the scientist knows that the South Sea atoll

is the work of countless, unseen coral builders, working below the surface of the sea.

And so I asked myself: "Is an idea, too, like this? Is it only the final result of a long series of unseen idea-building processes which go on beneath the surface of the conscious mind?

"If so, can these processes be identified, so that they can consciously be followed and utilized? In short, can a formula or technique be developed in answer to the question: How do you get ideas?"

What I now propose to you is the result of a long-time pondering of these questions and of close observation of the work of idea-producing men with whom I have had associations.

This has brought me to the conclusion that the production of ideas is just as definite a process as the production of Fords; that the production of ideas, too, runs on an assembly line; that in this production the mind follows an *operative technique* which can be learned and controlled; and that its effective use is just as much a matter of *practice in the technique* as is the effective use of any tool.

If you ask me why I am willing to give away the valuable formula of this discovery I will confide to you that experience has taught me two things about it:

First, the formula is so simple to state that few who hear it really believe in it.

Second, while simple to state, it actually requires the hardest kind of intellectual work to follow, so that not all who accept it use it.

Thus I broadcast this formula with no real fear of glutting the market in which I make my living.

The Pareto Theory

Now, we all know men of whom we have said: "He never had an idea in his life."

That saying brings us face to face with the first real question about this subject. Even assuming that there may be a technique for producing ideas, is everybody capable of using it? Or is there, in addition, some special ability for producing ideas which, after all, you must be born with—like a color sense or tone sense or card sense?

One answer to that question is suggested in the work *Mind and Society* by the great Italian sociologist Pareto.

Pareto thought that all the world could be

divided into two main types of people. These types he called, in the French in which he wrote, the *speculator* and the *rentier*.

In this classification *speculator* is a term used somewhat in the sense of our word "speculative," The *speculator* is the speculative type of person. And the distinguishing characteristic of this type, according to Pareto, is that he is *constantly preoccupied with the possibilities of new combinations*.

Please hold that italicized definition in mind, because we shall return to it later. Note particularly that word *pre-occupied*, with its brooding quality.

Pareto includes among the persons of this speculative type not only the business enterprisers—those who deal with financial and business schemes—but those engaged with inventions of every sort and with what he calls "political and diplomatic reconstructions."

In short, the type includes all those persons in any field who (like our President Roosevelt) can not let well enough alone and who speculate on how to change it.

The term used by Pareto to describe the other type, the *rentier*, is translated into English as the stockholder—though he sounds more like the bag holder to me. Such people, he says, are the routine, steady-going, unimaginative, conserving people, whom the *speculator* manipulates.

Whatever we may think of the adequacy of this theory of Pareto's as an entire explanation of social groups, I think we all recognize that these two types of human beings do exist. Whether they were born that way, or whether their environment and training made them that way, is beside the point. They *are*.

This being the case I suppose it must be true that there are large numbers of people whom no technique for producing ideas will ever help.

But it seems to me that the important point for our purpose is that the *speculators*, or reconstructors of this world, are a very large group. Theirs at least is the inherent capacity to produce ideas, and it is by no means such a rare capacity. And so, while perhaps not all God's chilluns got wings, enough have for each of us to hope that we may be among those that have.

At any rate, I propose to assume that if a man (or woman) is at all fascinated by advertising it is probably because he is among the reconstructors of this world. Therefore he has some creative powers; and these powers, like others, may be increased by making a deliberate effort to do so and by mastering a technique for their better use.

Training the Mind

Assuming, then, that we have some natural capacity for the creation of ideas, we come to the practical question: "What are the means of developing it?"

In learning any art the important things to learn are, first, Principles, and second, Method. This is true of the art of producing ideas.

Particular bits of knowledge are nothing, because they are made up of what Dr. Robert Hutchins once called *rapidly aging facts*. Principles and method are everything.

Thus in advertising we may know the names of types, how much engravings cost, what the rates and closing dates are in a thousand publications; we may know enough grammar and rhetoric to confound a schoolteacher and enough names of television artists to hold our own at a broadcaster's cocktail party; we may know all these things and still not be an advertising man, because we have no understanding of the principles and fundamental methods by which advertising works.

On the other hand, we may know none of these things but have insight into advertising principles and method, so that by employing technicians to help us we may produce advertising results. Thus we sometimes see a manufacturer or merchant who is a better advertising man than his advertising agent or manager.

So with the art of producing ideas. What is most valuable to know is not where to look for a particular idea, but how to train the mind in the *method* by which all ideas are produced and how to grasp the *principles* which are at the source of all ideas.

Combining Old Elements

With regard to the general principles which underlie the production of ideas, it seems to me that there are two which are important.

The first of these has already been touched upon in the quotation from Pareto: namely, that an idea is nothing more nor less than a new combination of old elements.

This is, perhaps, the most important fact in connection with the production of ideas. However, I want to leave the elaboration of it until we come to a discussion of method. Then we can see the importance of this fact more clearly, through the application of it.

The second important principle involved is that the capacity to bring old elements into new combinations depends largely on the ability to see relationships.

Here, I suspect, is where minds differ to the greatest degree when it comes to the production of ideas. To some minds each fact is a separate bit of knowledge. To others it is a link in a chain of knowledge. It has relationships and similarities. It is not so much a fact as it is an illustration of a general law applying to a whole series of facts.

An illustration of this might be taken from a relationship between advertising and psychiatry. At first blush it might be hoped that there is no relationship! But the psychiatrists have discovered the profound influence which words have in the lives of their patients—words as symbols of emotional experiences.

And now Dr. Harold Lasswell has carried over these word-symbol studies of the psychiatrists to the field of political action and shown how word-symbols are used with the same emotional force in propaganda.

To a mind which is quick to see relationships several ideas will occur, fruitful for advertising, about this use of words as symbols. Is this, then, why the change of one word in a headline can make as much as 50 percent difference in advertising response? Can words, studies as emotional symbols, yield better advertising education than words studied as parts of rhetoric? What is the one word-symbol which will best arouse the emotion with which I wish this particular advertisement to be charged? And so on.

The point is, of course, that when relationships of this kind are seen they lead to the extraction of a general principle. This general principle, when grasped, suggests the key to a new application, a new combination, and the result is an idea.

Consequently the habit of mind which leads to a search for relationships between facts becomes of the highest importance in the production of idea. Now this habit of mind can undoubtedly be cultivated. I venture to suggest that, for the advertising man, one of the best ways to cultivate it is by study in the social sciences. A book like Veblen's *Theory of the Leisure Class* or Riesman's *The Lonely Crowd*, therefore, becomes a better book about advertising than most books about advertising.

Ideas Are New Combinations

With these two general principles in mind—the principle that an idea is a new combination, and the principle that the ability to make new combinations is heightened by an ability to see relationships—with these in mind let us now look at the actual method or procedure by which ideas are produced.

As I said before, what I am now about to contend is that in the production of ideas the mind follows a method which is just as definite as the method by which, say, Fords are produced.

In other words, that there is a technique for the use of the mind for this purpose; that whenever an idea is produced this technique is followed, consciously or unconsciously; and that this technique can consciously be cultivated and the ability of the mind to produce ideas thereby increased.

This technique of the mind follows five steps. I am sure that you will all recognize them individually. But the important thing is to recognize their relationship and to grasp the fact that the mind follows these five steps in definite order—that by no possibility can one of them be taken before the preceding one is completed, if an idea is to be produced.

The first of these steps is for the mind to gather its raw material.

That, I am sure, will strike you as a simple and obvious truth. Yet it is really amazing to what degree this step is ignored in practice.

Gathering raw material in a real way is not as simple as it sounds. It is such a terrible chore that we are constantly trying to dodge it. The time that

Ideas Are New Combinations

ought to be spent in material gathering is spent in wool gathering. Instead of working systematically at the job of gathering raw material we sit around hoping for inspiration to strike us. When we do that we are trying to get the mind to take the fourth step in the idea-producing process while we dodge the preceding steps.

The materials which must be gathered are of two kinds: they are specific and they are general.

In advertising, the specific materials are those relating to the product and the people to whom you propose to sell it. We constantly talk about the importance of having an intimate knowledge of the product and the consumer, but in fact we seldom work at it.

This, I suppose, is because a real knowledge of a product, and of people in relation to it, is not easy to come by. Getting it is something like the process which was recommended to De Maupassant as the way to learn to write. "Go out into the streets of Paris," he was told by an older writer, "and pick out a cab driver. He will look to you very much like every other cab driver. But study him until you can describe him so that he is seen in your description to be an individual, different from every other cab driver in the world."

This is the real meaning of that trite talk about getting an intimate knowledge of a product and its consumers. Most of us stop too soon in the process of getting it. If the surface differences are not striking we assume that there are no differences. But if we go deeply enough, or far enough, we nearly always find that between every product and some consumers there is an individuality of relationship which may lead to an idea.

Thus, for example, I could cite you the advertising for a well-known soap. At first there appeared nothing to say about it that had not been said for many soaps. But a study was made of the relation of soap to skin and hair—a study which resulted in a fair-sized book on the subject. And out of this book came copy ideas for five years of advertising; ideas which multiplied the sales of this soap by ten in that period. This is what is meant by gathering specific materials.

Of equal importance with the gathering of these specific materials is the continuous process of gathering general materials.

Every really good creative person in advertising whom I have ever know has always had two noticeable characteristics. First, there was no subject under the sun in which he could not easily get interested—from, say, Egyptian burial customs to modern art. Every facet of life had fascination for him. Second, he was an extensive browser in all sorts of fields of information. For it is with the advertising man as with the cow: no browsing, no milk.

Now this gathering of general materials is important because this is where the previously stated principle comes in—namely, that an idea is nothing more nor less than a new combination of elements. In advertising an idea results from a new combination of *specific knowledge* about products and people with *general knowledge* about life and events.

The process is something like that which takes place in the kaleidoscope. The kaleidoscope, as you know, is an instrument which designers sometimes use in searching for new patterns. It has little pieces of colored glass in it, and when these are viewed through a prism they reveal all sorts of geometrical designs. Every turn of its crank shifts these bits of glass into a new relationship and reveals a new pattern. The mathematical possibilities of such new combinations in the kaleidoscope are enormous, and the greater the number of pieces of glass in it the greater become the possibilities for new and striking combinations.

So it is with the production of ideas for advertising—or anything else. The construction of an advertisement is the construction of a new pattern in this kaleidoscopic world in which we live. The more of the elements of that world which are stored away in that pattern-making machine, the mind, the more the chances are increased for the production of new and striking combinations, or ideas. Advertising students who get restless about the "practical" value of general college subjects might consider this.

This, then, is the first step in the technique of producing ideas: the gathering of materials. Part of it, you will see, is a current job and part of it is a life-long job. Before passing on to the next step there are two practical suggestions I might make about this material-gathering process.

The first is that if you have any sizable job of specific material gathering to do it is useful to learn the card-index method of doing it.

This is simply to get yourself a supply of those little 3 × 5 ruled white cards and use them to write down the items of specific information as you gather them. If you do this, one item to a card, after a while you can begin to classify them by sections of your subject. Eventually you will have a whole file box of them, neatly classified.

The advantage of this method is not merely in such things as bringing order into your work and disclosing gaps in your knowledge. It lies even more in the fact that it keeps you from shirking the material-gathering job and by forcing your mind to go through the expression of your material in writing really prepares it to perform its idea-producing processes.

The second suggestion is that for storing up certain kinds of general material some method of doing it like a scrapbook or file is useful.

You will remember the famous scrapbooks which appear throughout the Sherlock Holmes stories and how the master detective spent his spare time indexing and cross-indexing the odd bits of material he gathered there. We run across an enormous amount of fugitive material which can be grist to the idea-producer's mill—newspaper clippings, publication articles, and original

Ideas Are New Combinations

observations. Out of such material it is possible to build a useful source book of ideas.

Once I jotted in such a book the question: "Why does every man hope his first child will be a boy?" Five years later it became the headline and idea for one of the most successful advertisements I ever produced.

The Mental Digestive Process

Now, assuming that you have done a workmanlike job of gathering material—that you have really worked at the first step—what is the next part of the process that the mind must go through? It is the process of masticating these materials, as you would food that you are preparing for digestion.

This part of the process is harder to describe in concrete terms because it goes on entirely inside your head.

What you do is to take the different bits of material which you have gathered and feel them all over, as it were, with the tentacles of the mind. You take one fact, turn it this way and that, look

The Mental Digestive Process

at it in different lights, and feel for the meaning of it. You bring two facts together and see how they fit.

What you are seeking now is the relationship, a synthesis where everything will come together in a neat combination, like a jig-saw puzzle.

And here a strange element comes in. This is that facts sometimes yield up their meaning quicker when you do not scan them too directly, too literally. You remember the winged messenger whose wings could only be seen when glanced at obliquely? It is like that. In fact, it is almost like listening for the meaning instead of looking for it. When creative people are in this stage of the process they get their reputation for absent-mindedness.

As you go through this part of the process two things will happen. First, little tentative or partial ideas will come to you. Put these down on paper. Never mind how crazy or incomplete they seem: get them down. These are foreshadowings of the real idea that is to come, and expressing these in words forwards the process. Here again the little 3 × 5 cards are useful.

The second thing that will happen is that, by and by, you will get very tired of trying to fit your puzzle together. Let me beg of you not to get tired too soon. The mind, too, has a second wind. Go after at least this second layer of mental energy in this process. Keep trying to get one or more partial thoughts onto your little cards.

But after a while you will reach the hopeless stage. Everything is a jumble in your mind, with no clear insight anywhere. When you reach this point, if you have first really persisted in efforts to fit your puzzle together, then the second stage in the whole process is completed, and you are ready for the third one.

In this third stage you make absolutely no effort of a direct nature. You drop the whole subject and put the problem out of your mind as completely as you can.

The Mental Digestive Process

It is important to realize that this is just as definite and just as necessary a stage in the process as the two preceding ones. What you have to do at this time, apparently, is to turn the problem over to your unconscious mind and let it work while you sleep.

There is one thing you can do in this stage which will help both to put the problem out of consciousness and to stimulate the unconscious, creative processes.

You remember how Sherlock Holmes used to stop right in the middle of a case and drag Watson off to a concert? That was a very irritating procedure to the practical and literalminded Watson. But Conan Doyle was a creator and knew the creative processes.

So when you reach this third stage in the production of an idea, drop the problem completely and turn to whatever stimulates your imagination and emotions. Listen to music, go to the theater or movies, read poetry or a detective story.

In the first stage you have gathered your food. In the second you have masticated it well. Now the digestive process is on. Let it alone—but stimulate the flow of gastric juices.

"Constantly Thinking About It"

Now, if you have really done your part in these three stages of the process you will almost surely experience the fourth.

Out of nowhere the Idea will appear.

It will come to you when you are least expecting it—while shaving, or bathing, or most often when you are half awake in the morning. It may waken you in the middle of the night.

Here, for instance, is the way it happens according to Mary Roberts Rinehart. In her story "Miss Pinkerton" she makes this character say:

And it was while I was folding up that copy of the Eagle and putting it away for later reading that something came into my mind. I have had this happen before; I can puzzle over a thing until I am in a state of utter confusion, give it up, and then suddenly have the answer leap into my mind without any apparent reason.

And here again is the way it happened in the discovery of the half-tone printing process, as told by Mr. Ives, the inventor of it:

> While operating my photostereotype process in Ithaca I studied the problem of half-tone process [first step]. I went to bed one night in a state of brainfag over the problem [end of second and beginning of third step] and the instant that I woke in the morning [end of third step] saw before me, apparently projected on the ceiling,

the completely worked-out process and equipment in operation [fourth step].

This is the way ideas come: after you have stopped straining for them and have passed through a period of rest and relaxation from the search.

Thus the story about Sir Isaac Newton and his discovery of the law of gravitation is probably not the whole truth. You will remember that when a lady asked the famous scientist how he came to make the discovery he is said to have replied, "By constantly thinking about it."

It was by constantly thinking about it that he made the discovery possible. But I suspect that if we knew the full history of the case we should find that the actual solution came while he was taking a walk in the country.

The Final Stage

One more stage you have to pass through to complete the idea-producing process: the stage which might be called the cold, gray dawn of the morning after.

In this stage you have to take your little newborn idea out into the world of reality. And when you do you usually find that it is not quite the marvelous child it seemed when you first gave birth to it.

It requires a deal of patient working over to make most ideas fit the exact conditions, or the practical exigencies, under which they must work. And here is where many good ideas are lost. The idea man, like the inventor, is often not patient enough or practical enough to go through with this adapting part of the process. But it has to be done if you are to put ideas to work in a work-a-day world.

Do not make the mistake of holding your idea close to your chest at this stage. Submit it to the criticism of the judicious.

When you do, a surprising thing will happen. You will find that a good idea has, as it were, self-expanding qualities. It stimulates those who see it to add to it. Thus possibilities in it which you have overlooked will come to light.

This, then, is the whole process or method by which ideas are produced:

First, the gathering of raw materials—both the materials of your immediate problem and the materials which come from a constant enrichment of your store of general knowledge.

Second, the working over of these materials in your mind.

Third, the incubating stage, where you let something beside the conscious mind do the work of synthesis.

Fourth, the actual birth of the Idea—the "Eureka! I have it!" stage.

And fifth, the final shaping and development of the idea to practical usefulness.

Some After-Thoughts

Let me express my gratification at the number of letters which have come to me from readers of the earlier editions. The most gratifying have come from people who say "It works!"—that they have followed the prescription and gotten results.

Many have been from other creative people, entirely outside advertising—poets, painters, engineers, scientists, and even one writer of legal briefs—who say I have described their own experience. This supporting evidence will, I hope, encourage the beginner.

From my own further experience in advertising, government, and public affairs I find no essential points which I would modify in the idea-producing process. There is one, however, on which I would put greater emphasis. This is as to the store of *general* materials in the idea-producer's reservoir. I beg leave to illustrate this by a personal reference.

Some years ago I established my home in New Mexico and have been living there most of each year since. As a result I became interested in a whole new range of subjects, including Indian life, our Spanish history, native handicrafts, folkways of primitive people, etc.

Out of this grew some ideas about the possibilities of marketing some of the products of that region, by mail. I started with one of them—hand-woven neckties—wrote some advertisements about them, and copy-tested them. The result was a very tidy and interesting business.

The point is this: not only did the idea for starting the business come out of a general knowledge of the Southwest and its people, but all of the particular ideas for individual advertisements came from this source. If I had never gotten interested in Indian lore, Spanish-American history, the Spanish language, the handicraft philosophy, and so on, for their own sake, I would have had none of the reservoir of material which I believe made this advertising effective.

I have seen the truth of this principle a thousand times in practice. There are some advertisements you just cannot write until you have lived long enough—until, say, you have lived through certain experiences as a spouse, a parent, a businessman, or what not. The cycle of the years does something to fill your reservoir, unless you refuse to live spatially and emotionally.

But you can also enormously expand your experience, vicariously. It was the author of *Sard Harker*, I believe, who had never been to South America, yet wrote a corking good adventure book about it. I am convinced, however, that you gather this vicarious experience best, not when you are boning up on it for an immediate purpose, but when you are pursuing it as an end in itself.

Of course, if you consider that your education was finished when you left college and wouldn't be caught dead with a copy of, say, one of Jane Austen's novels under your pillow, go no farther. In that case you will probably never know how the landed gentry of nineteenth century England scorned people "in trade," nor have any ideas about why the Hudson River Squire strain in this country does the same. And that just possibly, some day, might keep you from producing a really effective series of "snob appeal" advertisements for the "carriage trade." Of course, this is a disappearing race, so maybe it doesn't matter.

But the principle of constantly expanding your experience, both personally and vicariously, does matter tremendously in any idea-producing job. Make no mistake about that.

Another point to encourage you. No doubt you

Some After-Thoughts

have seen people who seem to spark ideas—good ideas—right off the "top of their heads," without ever going through all this process which I have described.

Sometimes you have only seen the "Eureka! I have it!" stage take place. But sometimes you have also seen the fruits of long discipline in the practices here advocated. This discipline produces a mind so well stocked, and so quick at discerning relationships, as to be capable of such fast production.

Still another point I might elaborate on a little is about words. We tend to forget that words are, themselves, ideas. They might be called ideas in a state of suspended animation. When the words are mastered the ideas tend to come alive again.

Take the word *semantics*, for example. The chances are you will never use it in an advertisement. But if you have it in your vocabulary you will have a number of ideas about the use of words as symbols which will be of very practical value indeed. (If you don't have it in your vocabulary, look up Hayakawa's *Language in Thought and Action*.)

Thus, words being symbols of ideas, we can collect ideas by collecting words. The fellow who said he tried reading the dictionary but couldn't get the hang of the story simply missed the point: namely, that it is a collection of short stories.

And, finally, let me suggest a few other books which will expand your understanding of this whole idea-producing process:

The Art of Thought by Graham Walls. Published by Jonathan Cape, Ltd., London.

Science and Method by H. Poincaré. Translation by F. Maitland. Published by Thos. Nelson & Sons, London.

The Art of Scientific Investigation by W. I. B. Beveridge. A Modern Library paperback edition.

Word List

- 本文で使われている全ての語を掲載しています（LEVEL 1、2）。ただし、LEVEL 3 以上は、中学校レベルの語を含みません。
- 語形が規則変化する語の見出しは原形で示しています。不規則変化語は本文中で使われている形になっています。
- 一般的な意味を紹介していますので、一部の語で本文で実際に使われている品詞や意味と合っていないことがあります。
- 品詞は以下のように示しています。

名名詞	代代名詞	形形容詞	副副詞	動動詞	助助詞
前前置詞	接接続詞	間間投詞	冠冠詞	略略語	俗俗語
熟熟語	頭接頭語	尾接尾語	号記号	関関係代名詞	

A

- **ability** 名①できること、(〜する)能力 ②才能
- **absentmindedness** 名放心状態
- **absolutely** 副完全に、確実に、(yesを強調する返事として)そうですとも
- **accept** 動①〜を受け入れる ②〜に同意する、〜を認める
- **accident** 名①(不慮の)事故、災難 ②偶然
- **according** 副《- to》〜によれば[よると]
- **account** 名①説明(書) ②勘定 ③(銀行の)口座 動〜を…とみなす account for 〜 説明する、〜の責任を負う
- **active** 形①活動的な ②積極的な ③活動[作動]中の
- **actual** 形実際の、現実の
- **actually** 副実際に、本当に
- **ad** 略 advertisement (広告、宣伝)の略
- **adapt** 動〜に適合させる、順応させる
- **add** 動〜を(…に)加える、足す
- **addition** 名付加、追加 in addition 加えて、さらに
- **adequacy** 名妥当性、適切さ
- **advance** 名進歩、前進 動進む[進める]、進歩する[させる] 形先行の
- **advantage** 名有利な点[立場]、強み、優越
- **adventure** 名冒険 動危険を冒す
- **advertisement** 名広告、宣伝
- **advertising** 名広告、宣伝 形広告の
- **advocate** 名提唱者、支持者 動主張する、提唱する
- **affair** 名事柄、事件
- **After-Thought** 名追記
- **afterward** 副その後、のちに
- **agency** 名代理店、仲介
- **agent** 名①代理人 ②代表者
- **aging** 形年老いた、老朽化した 名老化、年老いること
- **Albert Einstein** アルバート・アインシュタイン《ドイツ出身の物理学者》
- **alleged** 形〜であるとされている、疑わしい、疑惑の
- **amazing** 形驚くべき、見事な

WORD LIST

- **America** 名アメリカ
- **American** 形アメリカの
- **amount** 名①量, 額 ②《the - 》(~の)合計 動(総計)~になる
- **analyze** 動分析する, 解析する
- **ancient** 形昔の, 古代の
- **anywhere** 副どこかへ[に], どこにも[へも], どこにでも
- **apparent** 形明らかな, 明白な, 見かけの, 外見上の
- **apparently** 副見たところ~らしい, 明らかに
- **appeal** 動①~を求める, ~を訴える ②(人の)気に入る 名①要求, 訴え ②魅力, 人気
- **appear** 動①現れる, 見えてくる ②(~のように)見える, ~らしい
- **appearance** 名①現れること, 出現 ②外見, 印象
- **application** 名①申し込み, 応募, 申込書 ②適用, 応用
- **apply** 動①申し込む, 志願する ②あてはまる ③~に適用する apply to ~ ~に適用する, ~に当てはまる, ~に問い合わせる
- **arouse** 動(感情などを)起こす, 刺激する
- **art** 名①芸術, 美術 ②技法, 術
- **article** 名①(法令・誓約などの)箇条, 項目 ②(新聞・雑誌などの)記事
- **artist** 名芸術家
- **assembly** 名①集合, 集めること, 会合 ②組み立て ③下院, 議会 assembly line 流れ作業
- **association** 名①交際, 連合, 結合 ②連想 ③協会, 組合
- **assume** 動①~と仮定する, ~を当然のことと思う ②~を引き受ける
- **assurance** 名確信, 保証, 保険
- **atoll** 名環礁
- **attention** 名①注意, 集中 ②配慮, 手当て 間《号令として》気をつけ
- **author** 名著者, 作家 動~を著作する, ~を創作する
- **available** 形利用(使用, 入手)できる, 得られる
- **await** 動待つ, 待ち受ける
- **awake** 動①目覚めさせる ②目覚める 形目が覚めて

B

- **bag holder** 鴨にされる人
- **basic** 形基礎の, 基本の 名《-s》基礎, 基本, 必需品
- **bathing** 名水浴び, 海水浴, 水泳 動 bath, bathe (風呂に入る, 水浴する)の現在分詞
- **beg** 動~を懇願する
- **beginner** 名初心者
- **belong** 動《- to》~に属する, ~のものである
- **below** 前①~より下に ②~以下の, ~より劣る 副下に[へ]
- **beneath** 前~の下に[の], ~より低い 副下に, 劣って
- **Bertrand Russell** バートランド・ラッセル《イギリスの数学者, 論理学者》
- **beside** 前①~のそばに, ~と並んで ②~と比べると ③~とはずれて
- **bill** 名①請求書, 勘定書 ②法案 ③紙幣 ④ビラ ⑤くちばし 動①~に請求書を送る ②~を勘定書に記入する
- **birth** 名①出産, 誕生 ②生まれ, 起源, (よい)家柄
- **bit** 名①《a - of》少しの~, 1つの~ ②小片 **a bit** 少し, ちょっと 動 bite (~をかむ)の過去, 過去分詞
- **blank** 形①白紙の, からの ②うつろな, 単調な 名空白, 空虚
- **blush** 動顔を赤らめる 名①赤面 ②赤色, バラ色 **at first blush** 一見

A Technique for Producing Ideas

したところ
- □ **bone** 名①骨,《-s》骨格 ②《-s》要点,骨組み 動(魚・肉)の骨をとる **bone up on** 懸命にする
- □ **brainfag** 形頭を働かせて
- □ **brand** 名ブランド,商標,品種
- □ **breath** 名①息,呼吸 ②《a-》(風の)そよぎ,気配,きざし **out of breath** 息を切らして
- □ **brief** 形①短い時間の ②簡単な 名①要点,概要 ②訴訟書類
- □ **broadcast** 名放送,番組 動放送する,広める 形放送の
- □ **broadcaster** 名放送局,アナウンサー
- □ **brooding** 形陰気な,ふさぎ込んだ
- □ **browser** 名①拾い読みする人,雑学家 ②ブラウザ
- □ **browsing** 名ざっと見ること,拾い読みすること,(動物などが草などを)食べること
- □ **burial** 名埋葬
- □ **businessman** 名ビジネスマン,実業家
- □ **by and by** 熟やがて,段々
- □ **by no means** 熟決して~ではない

C

- □ **cab** 名タクシー
- □ **call one's attention** 熟注意を促す
- □ **capable** 形能力がある,有能な
- □ **capacity** 名①定員,容量 ②能力,(潜在的な)可能性
- □ **card-index** 名カード索引
- □ **carriage** 名①馬車 ②乗り物,車 **carriage trade** 上得意様,金持ち
- □ **carry over** 熟引き継がれる
- □ **ceiling** 名天井
- □ **certain** 形①確実な,必ず~する ②(人が)確信した ③ある ④いくらかの 代~の中のいくつか
- □ **chairman** 名委員長,会長,議長
- □ **character** 名①個性 ②(小説・劇などの)登場人物 ③文字,記号
- □ **characteristic** 名特徴,特性
- □ **charge** 動①(代金)を請求する ②(…を)~に負わせる 名①請求金額,料金 ②責任 ③非難,告発
- □ **chart** 名表,図表,カルテ 動図で示す,図表にする
- □ **check** 動①~を照合する,~を検査する ②~を阻止[妨害]する ③(所持品)を預ける 名①照合,検査 ②小切手 ③(突然の)停止,阻止(するもの) ④伝票,勘定書
- □ **chemist** 名①化学者,生化学者 ②薬屋,薬剤師
- □ **chest** 名①大きな箱,戸棚,たんす ②金庫 ③胸心,肺
- □ **Chicago** 名シカゴ《米国の都市》
- □ **chief** 名頭,長,親分 形最高位の,第一の,主要な
- □ **chilluns** 名(神の)申し子 **God's chilluns got wings**《黒人霊歌の一句》神の申し子である人間は翼をもっている
- □ **chore** 名雑用,雑役 動雑用をする
- □ **cite** 動~に言及する,~を引用する 名言及,引用
- □ **classification** 名分類,等級,区分
- □ **classify** 動~を分類する,~を区別する
- □ **clear** 形①はっきりした,明白な ②澄んだ ③(よく)晴れた 動①~をはっきりさせる ②~を片づける ③晴れる 副①はっきりと ②すっかり,完全に
- □ **clearly** 副①明らかに,はっきりと ②《返答に用いて》そのとおり
- □ **clipping** 名切り抜き,クリッピング
- □ **closing date** 締切日

46

WORD LIST

- **cocktail** 名カクテル
- **collection** 名収集, 収蔵物
- **combination** 名①結合(状態, 行為), 団結 ②連合, 同盟
- **combine** 動①結合する[させる] ②連合する, 協力する 名合同, 連合
- **come by** 熟手に入れる, 立ち寄る, 考える, (被害などを)受ける
- **come up with** 熟思いつく
- **come to** 熟〜に達する
- **comfort** 名①快適さ, 満足 ②慰め ③安楽 動〜を心地よくする
- **communication** 名伝えること, 伝導, 連絡
- **complete** 形完全な, 全くの, 完成した 動〜を完成させる
- **completely** 副完全に, すっかり
- **Conan Doyle** コナン・ドイル《イギリスの作家》
- **concert** 名①音楽[演奏]会, コンサート ②一致, 協力
- **concise** 形簡潔な, 簡明な
- **conclusion** 名結論, 結末
- **concrete** 形具体的な, 明確な 名コンクリート
- **condition** 名①(健康)状態, 境遇 ②(-s)状況, 様子 ③条件 動〜を適応させる, 〜を条件づける
- **confide** 動〜を信頼する, 〜を信用する, (秘密などを)打ち明ける
- **confound** 動〜を困惑させる, 〜を混乱させる, 〜をのろう
- **confusion** 名混乱(状態)
- **connection** 名①つながり, 関係 ②縁故
- **conscious** 形①(状況などを)意識している, 自覚している ②意識のある 名意識
- **consciously** 副意識して, 自覚して, 故意に
- **consciousness** 名意識, 自覚, 気づいていること
- **consequently** 副したがって, 結果として
- **conserve** 動保存する, 保護する
- **consider** 動①考慮する ②(〜と)みなす ③〜を気にかける, 思いやる
- **constant** 形①絶えない, 一定の, 不変の ②不屈の, 確固たる 名定数
- **constantly** 副絶えず, いつも, 絶え間なく
- **construction** 名構造, 建設, 工事, 建物
- **consumer** 名消費者
- **contend** 動〜と争う, 〜と競う, 〜と論争する, 強く主張する
- **content** 名①《-s》中身, 内容, 目次 ②満足 形満足して 動満足する[させる]
- **continuous** 形連続的な, 継続する, 途切れない
- **control** 動①〜を管理[支配]する ②〜を抑制する 名①管理, 支配(力) ②抑制
- **convey** 動①〜を運ぶ ②〜を伝達する, 〜を伝える ③〜を譲渡する
- **convince** 動納得させる, 確信させる
- **copy** 名①コピー ②(書籍の)一部, 冊 ③広告文 動〜を写す, まねる
- **copy-test** 動コピーテストする
- **coral** 名サンゴ 形サンゴの coral builder サンゴ虫
- **corking** 形素晴らしい, すてきな 副とても, 非常に
- **cost** 名①値段, 費用 ②損失, 犠牲 動(金, 費用)がかかる, 〜を要する
- **countless** 形無数の, 数えきれない
- **cow** 名雌牛, 乳牛
- **craft** 名①技術, 技巧 ②船, 飛行機 動高い技術で(精巧に)作る
- **crank** 名クランク(エンジンを動かす道具), 変り者, 気まぐれ 動クランクを回す

A Technique for Producing Ideas

- **crazy** 形①狂気の, ばかげた, 無茶な ②夢中の, 熱狂的な
- **creation** 名創造[物]
- **creative** 形創造的な, 独創的な
- **creator** 名創作者, 創造者, 神
- **criticism** 名批評, 批判, 評論, 酷評
- **cross-indexing** 名別の角度からの索引付け
- **crowd** 動群がる, 混雑する 名群集, 雑踏, 多数
- **cultivate** 動耕す, 栽培する, (才能などを)養う, 育成する
- **current** 形現在の, 目下の, 通用[流通]している 名流れ, 電流, 風潮
- **cutting edge** ①刃先 ②最前線
- **cycle** 名①周期, 循環 ②自転車, オートバイ 動①自転車に乗る, 自転車旅行をする ②循環する

D

- **dandy** 名しゃれ男 形おしゃれな, 極上の
- **dawn** 名①《無冠詞で》夜明け ②《the-》初め, きざし 動①(夜が)明ける ②(真実などが)わかり始める
- **DDB Worldwide** DDBワールドワイド《アメリカの広告代理店》
- **deal** 動①〜を分配する ②《-with [in]》〜を扱う 名①取引, 扱い ②(不特定の)量, 額
- **deeply** 副深く, 非常に
- **definite** 形限定された, 明確な, はっきりした
- **definition** 名定義, 限定
- **degree** 名①程度, 階級, 位, 身分 ②(温度・角度の)度
- **deliberate** 形よく考えた, 慎重な, 意図的な 動〜を熟考する, 〜を議論する
- **demand** 動①〜を要求する ②〜を必要とする 名①要求, 請求 ②需要
- **department** 名①部門, 課, 局, 担当分野 ②《D-》(米国・英国の)省
- **depend** 動《-on [upon]》①〜を頼る, 〜をあてにする ②〜による
- **describe** 動〜を(言葉で)描写する, 〜の特色を述べる, 〜を説明する
- **description** 名(言葉で)記述(すること), 描写(すること)
- **design** 動〜を設計する, 〜を企てる 名デザイン, 設計(図)
- **designer** 名デザイナー, 設計者
- **detail** 名①細部, 《-s》詳細 ②《-s》個人情報 動〜を詳しく述べる
- **detective** 名探偵, 刑事 形探偵の
- **develop** 動①発達する[させる] ②〜を開発する
- **development** 名①発達, 発展 ②展開
- **dictionary** 名辞書, 辞典
- **differ** 動異なる, 違う, 意見が合わない
- **digest** 動〜を消化する, 〜を要約する 名要約, ダイジェスト, 消化
- **digestion** 名消化, 理解
- **digestive** 形消化の, 消化を助ける 名消化剤
- **diplomatic** 形外交(上)の, 外交官の
- **direct** 形まっすぐな, 直接の, 率直な 副まっすぐに, 直接に 動①〜を指導する, 〜を監督する ②(目・注意・努力など)を向ける
- **directly** 副①じかに ②まっすぐに ③ちょうど
- **director** 名管理者, 指導者, 監督
- **disappear** 動見えなくなる, 姿を消す, なくなる
- **discern** 動〜を見分ける, 〜を識別する
- **discipline** 名規律, しつけ 動訓練する, しつける

WORD LIST

- **disclose** 動(秘密などを)公表する, 暴露する
- **discovery** 名発見
- **discuss** 動~を議論[検討]する
- **discussion** 名討議, 討論
- **distinguishing** 形特徴的な
- **divide** 動分かれる[分ける], 割れる[割る]
- **dodge** 動さっと身をかわす, さっと隠れる, (質問を)そらす 名身をかわすこと, ごまかし
- **doubt** 名疑い, 不確かなこと 動~を疑う
- **Doyle Dane** ドイル・デーン《人名》
- **Dr.** ~博士, 《医者に対して》~先生
- **drag** 動①~を引きずる ②のろのろ動く 名①引きずること ②のろのろすること drag off ひっぱり出して
- **dramatic** 形劇的な, 印象的な, 劇の
- **driver** 名①運転手 ②(馬車の)御者

E

- **eagle** 名ワシ《E-》ワシ座
- **earn** 動①(金)を儲ける, 稼ぐ ②(名声)を博す earn ones living 生計を立てる
- **easily** 副①容易に, たやすく, 苦もなく ②気楽に
- **edge** 名①刃 ②端, 縁 動①~に刃をつける, ~を鋭くする ②~を縁どる, 縁に沿って進む
- **edition** 名(書籍・新聞の)版
- **education** 名教育, 教養
- **effective** 形効果的である, 有効である
- **effort** 名努力(の成果)
- **Egyptian** 名エジプト人, エジプト語 形エジプト人の, エジプト語の
- **elaborate** 形念入りな, 手の込んだ 動~を念入りに作る, 考えを練る
- **elaboration** 名念入りに作ること, 入念さ, 綿密さ, 詳細
- **element** 名要素, 成分, 元素
- **emerge** 動現れる, 浮かび上がる, 明らかになる
- **emotion** 名感激, 感動, 感情
- **emotional** 形感情的な, 感激しやすい
- **emotionally** 副感情的に, 情緒的に
- **emphasis** 名強調, 強勢, 重要性 put emphasis 重点を置く, 強調する
- **employ** 動(人)を雇う[使う], ~を利用する 名雇用, 職業
- **encounter** 動~に(思いがけなく)出会う 名遭遇, (思いがけない)出会い
- **encourage** 動①~を勇気づける ②~を促進する, ~を助長する
- **engage** 動①~を約束する, ~と婚約する ②~を雇う, 従事する[させる]
- **engineer** 名技師
- **England** 名①イングランド ②英国
- **engraving** 名彫刻, 版画, 印刷物, 製版
- **enormous** 形莫大な, 非常に大きい, 巨大な
- **enormously** 副非常に, 巨大に, ものすごく, 法外に
- **enrichment** 名豊かにすること, 価値を高めること, 栄養価を高めること, 濃縮
- **enterpriser** 名企業家
- **enthusiasm** 名情熱, 熱意, 熱心
- **entire** 形全体の, 完全な, 全くの
- **entirely** 副完全に, 全く
- **environment** 名環境, 周囲
- **equal** 形等しい, 均等な, 平等な 動~に匹敵する, 等しい

- □ **equipment** 名①装置, 機材, 道具 ②身につけているもの, 知識, 資質
- □ **essential** 形本質的な, 必須の 名本質, 要点, 必需品
- □ **establish** 動〜を確立する, 〜を立証する, 〜を設置[設立]する
- □ **etc** 略〜など, その他
- □ **eureka** 間(探していたものなどが)見つかった！分かった！《語源はギリシア語》
- □ **eventually** 副結局は
- □ **everybody** 代誰でも, 皆
- □ **everything** 代すべてのこと[もの], 何でも, 何もかも
- □ **evidence** 名①証拠, 証人 ②形跡
- □ **exact** 形正確な, 厳密な, きちょうめんな
- □ **executive** 形実行の, 執行の 名①高官, 実行委員 ②重役, 役員, 幹部
- □ **exigency** 名①緊急事態, 危急 ②要求, 要件
- □ **exist** 動存在する, 生存する, ある
- □ **expand** 動広げる, 拡張(大)する
- □ **expect** 動〜を予期[予測]する, (当然のこととして)〜を期待する
- □ **explanation** 名①説明, 解説, 釈明 ②解釈, 意味
- □ **express** 動〜を表現する, 〜を述べる 形①明白な ②急行の 名速達便, 急行列車 副速達で, 急行で
- □ **expression** 名①表現, 表示, 表情 ②言い回し, 語句
- □ **extensive** 形広い, 広範囲にわたる, 大規模な
- □ **extraction** 名①抽出, 抜き取り, 引用, 摘出 ②生まれ, 素性

F

- □ **facet** 名(宝石などの)小面, (物事の)面
- □ **face to face** 熟面と向かっての, 〜に直面して
- □ **fair-sized** 形かなり多額の, かなりの量(大きさ)の
- □ **farther** 副もっと遠く, さらに先に 形もっと向こうの, さらに進んだ
- □ **fascinate** 動〜を魅惑する, 〜をうっとりさせる
- □ **fascination** 名魅惑, 魅力, うっとりした状態
- □ **fear** 名①恐れ ②心配, 不安 動①〜を恐れる ②〜を心配する
- □ **fellow** 名①仲間, 同僚 ②人, やつ 形仲間の, 同士の
- □ **file** 名ファイル, 書類綴じ, 縦列 動とじ込む, 保管する
- □ **final** 形最後の, 決定的な 名①最後のもの ②《-s》決勝戦, 最終試験
- □ **financial** 形①財務上の, 金融上の ②金融関係者の
- □ **fit** 形①適当な, 相応な ②体の調子がよい 動合致[適合]する[させる] 名発作, けいれん, 一時的興奮
- □ **flatter** 動①お世辞をいう, おおげさにほめる ②《be -ed》うれしく[光栄に]思う
- □ **flesh** 名肉, 《the –》肉体
- □ **flow** 動流れ出る, あふれる 名流出, 流ちょう(なこと)
- □ **fold** 名折り目, ひだ 動①〜を折りたたむ, 〜を包む ②(手)を組む
- □ **folkway** 名《-s》風俗, 風習, しきたり
- □ **follower** 名信奉者, 追随者
- □ **force** 名力, 勢い 動〜に強制する, 力づくで〜する
- □ **Ford** 名フォード社《自動車メーカー》, フォード型自動車
- □ **foreshadowing** 名兆候, 前兆
- □ **foreword** 名(本などの)前書き, 序文
- □ **form** 名①形, 形式 ②書式 動〜を

Word List

- 形づくる
- **formula** 图公式, 方式, 一定の形式, きまり文句
- **forward** 形①前方の, 前方へ向かう ②将来の ③先の 副①前方に ②将来に向けて ③先へ, 進んで 動①〜を転送する ②〜を進める 图前衛
- **French** 形フランス(人[語])の 图フランス語, 《the −》フランス人
- **from here on** 熟今後
- **fruitful** 形実り多い, 多産な, 充実した, 有益な
- **fugitive** 形つかの間の, 変わりやすい 图逃亡者
- **fundamental** 图基本, 原理 形基本の, 根本的な, 重要な
- **funny** 形①おもしろい, こっけいな ②奇妙な, うさんくさい
- **further** 形いっそう遠い, その上の, なおいっそうの 副いっそう遠く, その上に, もっと 動〜を促進する

G

- **gap** 图ギャップ, 隔たり, 隙間 動すき間ができる
- **gastric** 形胃の gastric juice 胃液
- **gather** 動①集まる[集める] ②生じる, 増す ③〜を推測する
- **gene** 图遺伝子
- **general** 形①全体の, 一般の, 普通の ②おおよその 图大将, 将軍
- **gentry** 图①貴族, 上流階級 ②連中
- **geometrical** 形幾何(学)的な
- **get tired** 熟疲れる, 飽きる
- **get to the heart** 熟核心にふれる
- **giant** 图①巨人, 大男 ②巨匠 形巨大な, 偉大な
- **give away** 熟提供する, 譲歩する, (秘密を)明かす・暴露する, (正体を)現す

- **glance** 图①ちらっと見ること, 一べつ ②ひらめき ③かすめること 動①ちらりと見る ②かすめる
- **glut** 图供給過剰 動過剰に供給する, 食べ過ぎる
- **gotten** 動 get (〜を得る)の過去分詞
- **government** 图政治, 政府, 支配
- **graduate** 動〜を卒業する 图卒業生, (〜学校の)出身者 形卒業した graduate student 大学院生
- **Graham Walls** グラハム・ウォールズ《人名》
- **grammar** 图文法
- **grasp** 動〜をつかむ, 握る, とらえる, 〜を理解する 图把握, 理解(力)
- **gratification** 图満足, 喜び
- **gratify** 動〜を満足させる, 〜を喜ばす
- **gravitation** 图重力, 引力 law of gravitation 引力の法則
- **grist** 图①製粉用穀物, 穀粉 ②価値あるもの grist to one's mill もうけ口, 利益の種
- **guarantee** 图保証, 保証書, 保証人 動保証する, 請け合う
- **guidance** 图案内, 手引き

H

- **habit** 图習慣, 癖, 気質
- **half-tone** 图網版 形網版の, 中間調の
- **hand-woven** 形手織りの
- **handicraft** 图手工芸(品), 手先の器用さ
- **hang** 動かかる[かける], 〜をつるす, ぶら下がる 图かかり具合
- **Harold Lasswell** ハロルド・ラスウェル《人名》
- **Hayakawa** 图ハヤカワ《人名》

A Technique for Producing Ideas

- **headline** 名(新聞等の)見出し
- **hearty** 形①心のこもった, 親切な ②本心からの
- **heighten** 動①強める, 高じさせる ②～を高くする
- **helpful** 形役に立つ, 参考になる
- **holder** 名所有者, 容器, 入れ物
- **hopeless** 形①希望のない, 絶望的な ②勝ち目のない
- **however** 副たとえ～でも 接けれども, だが
- **Hudson River Squire** ハドソン川流域紳士
- **hung** 動 hang (かかる[かける])の過去, 過去分詞

I

- **idea-building** 形アイデア形成の
- **idea-producer** 名アイデアを作る人
- **idea-producing** 形アイデア作成の
- **identify** 動①～を(本人, 同一と)確認する, 見分ける ②意気投合する
- **ignore** 動無視する, 忘る
- **illuminate** 形(問題などを)解明する, 明るくする
- **illustrate** 動～を説明する, ～を明らかにする, さし絵を入れる
- **illustration** 名さし絵, 図解, 説明
- **imagination** 名想像(力), 空想
- **immediate** 形さっそくの, 即座の, 直接の
- **immediately** 副すぐに, ～するやいなや
- **importance** 名重要性, 大切さ
- **impress** 動～を印象づける, ～を感銘させる 名刻印, こん跡
- **improve** 動改善する[させる], 進歩する
- **Inc.** 略《incorporatedの略》株式会社
- **include** 動～を含む, ～を勘定に入れる
- **incomparable** 形比類のない, 比較にならない, ずば抜けた
- **incomplete** 形不完全な, 不十分な, 未完成の
- **increase** 動増加[増強]する[させる] 名増加(量), 増大
- **incubate** 動(卵などが)孵化する
- **indebted** 形借金がある, 恩を受けている
- **indeed** 副実際, 本当に,《強意》全く 間本当に, まさか
- **indexing** 名索引付け
- **Indian** 名①インド人 ②(アメリカ)インディアン《今は通例 Native American》 形①インドの, インド人の ②(アメリカ)インディアンの
- **individual** 形独立した, 個性的な, 個々の 名①個体, 個人
- **individuality** 名個性, 特性, 個人
- **individually** 副個人的に, 一つ一つ
- **inexpensively** 形費用をかけず, 安く
- **influence** 名影響, 勢力 動～に影響をおよぼす
- **informal** 形形式張らない, 非公式の
- **inherent** 形固有の, 特有の, 生まれつきの
- **insight** 名洞察, 真相, 見識
- **inspiration** 名霊感, ひらめき, 妙案, 吸気
- **inspire** 動①奮い立たせる, 感動させる ②(人に)生じさせる
- **instance** 名①例 ②場合, 事実 ③請求, 依頼 for instance 例えば 動～を例としてあげる
- **instant** 形即時の, 緊急の, 即席の

Word List

- 名瞬間, 寸時
- **instead** 副その代わりに instead of ~ ~の代わりに, ~をしないで
- **instrument** 名①道具, 器具, 器械 ②楽器 ③手段
- **intellectual** 形知的な, 知性のある 名知識人, 有識者
- **in the first place** 熟そもそも, 第一に
- **intimate** 形親密な, (事情などに)詳しい, (男女が)肉体関係にある 名親友
- **intimidating** 形脅威的な, 威嚇するような, おびえさせる
- **intuition** 名直感, 洞察
- **inventor** 名発明者, 発案者
- **investigation** 名(徹底的な)調査, 取り調べ
- **involve** 動①~を含む, 伴う ②巻き込む, かかわらせる
- **irritating** 形イライラさせる, 腹の立つ
- **Isaac Newton** アイザック・ニュートン《英国の物理学者・天文学者》
- **Italian** 名イタリア人, イタリア語 形イタリアの
- **italicize** 動イタリック体で印刷する, イタリック体にする
- **item** 名①項目, 品目 ②(新聞などの)記事
- **Ithaca** 名イサカ《地名》
- **itself** 代それ自体, それ自身
- **Ives** 名アイヴズ《人名》

J

- **Jane Austen** ジェーン・オースティン《イギリスの作家》
- **jig-saw** 名ジグソー, 糸のこ, ジグソーパズル
- **Jonathan Cape** ジョナサン・ケープ《人名》
- **jot** 動~をさっと書き留める, ~をメモする 名わずか, 微少
- **judicious** 形思慮分別のある, 賢明な
- **jumble** 名ごちゃ混ぜ, 混乱 動~がゴチャゴチャになる

K

- **kaleidoscope** 名万華鏡
- **kaleidoscopic** 形万華鏡のような, 目まぐるしく変わる
- **Keith Reinhard** キース・ラインハルト《人名》
- **knowledge** 名知識, 理解, 学問
- **Kobler** 名コブラー《人名》

L

- **laid** 動lay (~を置く, ~を整える, 卵を産む)の過去, 過去分詞 laid down 築く, 敷設する
- **largely** 副大いに, 主として
- **layer** 名層, 重ね 動層になる[する]
- **leap** 動①跳ぶ ②~を跳び越える 名跳ぶこと
- **least** 形一番小さい, 最も少ない 副一番小さく, 最も少なく 名最小[少]
- **legal** 形法律(上)の, 正当な
- **leisure** 名余暇, 自由時間
- **lend** 動(~を)貸す, 与える
- **less** 形~より小さい[少ない] 副~より少なく, ~ほどでなく 名より少ない数[量・額]
- **lie** 動①うそをつく ②横たわる, 寝る ③(ある状態に)ある, 存在する 名うそ, 詐欺
- **life-long** 形一生の, 生涯の
- **link** 名①(鎖の)輪 ②リンク 動(~

A Technique for Producing Ideas

に, と)連結する, つながる
- [ ] **list** 名 名簿, 目録, 一覧表 動 ～を名簿[目録]に記入する
- [ ] **literally** 副 文字どおり, そっくりそのまま
- [ ] **literalminded** 形 想像力の乏しい, 現実的な考え方の
- [ ] **literature** 名 文学, 文芸, 参考文献
- [ ] **London** 名 ロンドン《イギリスの首都》
- [ ] **lonely** 形 ①孤独な, 心寂しい ②ひっそりした, 人里離れた *The Lonely Crowd*『孤独な群衆』
- [ ] **long-time** 形 長年の, 長い間の, 昔からの
- [ ] **lore** 名 言い伝え, 知識, (民間)伝承
- [ ] **lovely** 形 愛らしい, 美しい, すばらしい
- [ ] **Ltd.** 略《limitedの略》(会社が)有限責任の
- [ ] **lucidly** 副 明白に, 明快に

M

- [ ] **made up of** 熟《be-》～で構成されている, ～でできている
- [ ] **magic** 名 ①魔法, 手品 ②魔力
- [ ] **main** 形 ①主な, 主要な
- [ ] **Maitland** 名 メートランド《人名》
- [ ] **make one's living** 熟 生計を立てている, 自活する
- [ ] **manager** 名 経営者, 支配人, 支店長, 部長
- [ ] **manipulate** 動 操る, 操作する, 巧みに扱う
- [ ] **manufacturer** 名 製造業者, メーカー
- [ ] **mariner** 名 水夫, 船員
- [ ] **marvelous** 形 驚くべき, すばらしい
- [ ] **Mary Roberts Rinehart** メアリー・ロバーツ・ラインハート《人名》
- [ ] **master** 名 主人, 雇い主, 師 動 ①～を修得する ②～の主となる
- [ ] **masticate** 動 かむ, かみくだく
- [ ] **material** 形 ①物質の, 肉体的な ②不可欠な, 重要な 名 材料, 原料
- [ ] **material-gathering** 形 資料集めの
- [ ] **mathematical** 形 数学の, 数理的な, 正確な
- [ ] **Maupassant** 名 モーパッサン《人名》
- [ ] **means** 名 方法, 手段
- [ ] **mental** 形 ①心の, 精神の, 知能[知性]の ②暗算の
- [ ] **merchant** 名 商人, 貿易商
- [ ] **merely** 副 単に, たかが～に過ぎない
- [ ] **messenger** 名 使者, (伝言・小包などの)配達人, 伝達者
- [ ] **method** 名 ①方法, 手段 ②秩序, 体系
- [ ] **middle** 名 中間, 最中 形 中間の, 中央の
- [ ] **might** 動 ①～かもしれない ②～してもよい ③～できる
- [ ] **mill** 名 ①製造所 ②ミル, ひき機 動 ～をひく
- [ ] **mind** 名 ①心, 精神 ②知性 動 ①～を嫌だと思う ②～に気をつける, ～を用心する
- [ ] **modern** 形 現代[近代]の, 現代的な, 最近の 名 現代人
- [ ] **modify** 動 ～を修正する, ～を変更する, ～を加減する
- [ ] **moment** 名 ①瞬間, ちょっとの間 ②(特定の)時, 時期
- [ ] **multiply** 動 掛け算をする, ～が増える, ～を増やす, ～が繁殖する
- [ ] **mysterious** 形 神秘的な, 謎めいた

WORD LIST

N

- **naive** 形 世間知らずの, 無邪気な, 初心者の 名 うぶな人
- **namely** 副 すなわち, つまり
- **native** 形 ①出生(地)の, 自国の ②(〜に)固有の, 生まれつきの, 天然の 名 (ある土地に)生まれた人
- **nearly** 副 ①近くに, 親しく ②ほとんど, あやうく
- **neat** 形 きちんとした, きれいな
- **neatly** 副 きちんと, 巧妙に
- **necessary** 形 必要な, 必然の 名 《-s》必要品, 必需品
- **necktie** 名 ネクタイ
- **Nelson & Sons** ネルソン&サンズ《社名》
- **newborn** 形 生まれたばかりの 名 新生児
- **New Mexico** ニュー・メキシコ《地名》
- **newspaper** 名 新聞(紙)
- **none** 代 〜の何も[誰も, 少しも]…ない
- **nor** 接 〜もまたない neither 〜 nor … 〜も…もない
- **notably** 副 著しく, 目だって
- **note** 名 ①メモ, 覚書 ②注釈 ③注意, 注目 ④手形 動 ①〜を書き留める ②〜に注意[注目]する
- **noticeable** 形 人目を引く, 目立つ, 著しい
- **novel** 名 (長編)小説 形 新奇な, ざん新な
- **nowhere** 副 どこにも〜ない

O

- **obliquely** 副 斜めに, 遠まわしに
- **observation** 名 観察(力), 注目
- **obvious** 形 明らかな, 明白な
- **obviously** 副 明らかに, はっきりと
- **occur** 動 (事が)起こる, 生じる, (考えなどが)浮かぶ
- **odd** 形 ①奇妙な ②奇数の ③(一対のうちの)片方の
- **off and on** 熟 時おり, 断続して
- **offer** 動 (〜を)申し出る, (〜を)申し込む, (〜を)提供する 名 提案, 提供
- **officer** 名 役人, 公務員, 警察官
- **onto** 前 〜の上へ
- **operate** 動 ①(機械などが)動く, 〜を運転する, 〜を管理する ②作用する ③手術する
- **operation** 名 ①操作, 作業, 動作 ②経営, 軍事行動 ③手術
- **operative** 形 働いている, 作用している, 効力のある 名 職人, 探偵
- **original** 形 ①始めの, 元の, 本来の ②独創的な 名 原型, 原文
- **ought** 助 《- to》当然〜すべきである, きっと〜するはずである
- **outline** 名 ①外形, 輪郭 ②概略
- **overlook** 動 〜を見落とす, 〜を見逃す, (チャンスなどを)逃す

P

- **painter** 名 画家, ペンキ屋
- **paperback** 名 ペーパーバック 形 ペーパーバック(の)
- **Pareto** 名 パレート《人名》
- **Paris** 名 パリ《フランスの首都》
- **partial** 形 ①一部分の, 不公平な ②特に好きな
- **particular** 形 ①特別の ②詳細な 名 事項, 細部, 《-s》詳細
- **particularly** 副 特に, とりわけ
- **path** 名 ①(踏まれてできた)小道, 歩道 ②進路, 通路

A Technique for Producing Ideas

- **patient** 形我慢[忍耐]強い、根気のある 名病人、患者
- **pattern** 名①柄、型、模様 ②手本、模範 動①~を手本にする ②~に模様をつける
- **pattern-making** 形パターンを製造する
- **Peña Blanca** ペニャブランカ《地名》
- **perform** 動①(任務などを)行なう[果たす]、実行する ②~を演じる、演奏する
- **perhaps** 副たぶん、ことによると 名偶然のこと、仮定
- **period** 名期、期間、時代 形時代物の
- **persist** 動①固執する、主張する ②続く、存続する persist in~ ~に固執する
- **personal** 形①個人の ②本人自らの ③容姿の
- **personally** 副個人的には、自分で
- **philosophy** 名哲学、主義、信条、人生観
- **photostereotype** 名ステロ写真版
- **pick out** 熟拾い出す、見つけ出す、選ぶ
- **pillow** 名まくら
- **Pinkerton** 名ピンカートン《人名》
- **poet** 名詩人、歌人
- **poetry** 名詩歌、詩を書くこと
- **Poincare** 名ポアンカレ《人名》
- **political** 形①政治(上)の ②国家の、国政の ③政党の
- **ponder** 動じっくり考える、熟考する ponder on~ ~を熟慮する
- **possibility** 名可能性、見込み、将来性
- **possible** 形可能な、あり[起こり]得る
- **possibly** 副①あるいは、たぶん ②《否定文、疑問文で》どうしても、できる限り、とても、なんとか
- **practical** 形①実際的な、実用的な、役に立つ ②経験を積んだ
- **practitioner** 名実行者、開業者、開業医、弁護士
- **pre-occupied** 形夢中になった、気をとられている、うわの空の、先取りされた
- **preceding** 形先行する、先立つ、前の
- **prefatory** 形序文の、前置きの、前口上の
- **pre-occupied** 形夢中になった、気をとられている、うわの空の、先取りされた
- **prescription** 名規定、処方、処方せん、処方薬、時効
- **president** 名①大統領 ②社長、(大学の)学長、頭取
- **previously** 副前もって、あらかじめ、以前に
- **primitive** 形原始の、初期の、旧式の 名原始人、原始主義 primitive people 原住民
- **principle** 名①原理、原則 ②道義、正道
- **prism** 名プリズム、角柱
- **probably** 副たぶん、あるいは
- **procedure** 名手順、手続き
- **process** 名①過程、経過、進行 ②手順、方法、製法、加工
- **product** 名①製品、産物 ②成果、結果
- **production** 名製造、生産
- **professional** 形専門の、プロの、職業的な 名専門家、プロ
- **profound** 形深い、深遠な、心の底から、難解な
- **project** 名計画、企画、事業
- **propaganda** 名(主義・思想の)宣伝、組織的な宣伝活動

WORD LIST

- **properly** 副 適切に, きっちりと
- **propose** 動①〜を申し込む, 〜を提案する ②結婚を申し込む
- **prove** 動①〜を証明する ②〜であることがわかる, 〜となる
- **psychiatrist** 名 精神科医
- **psychiatry** 名 精神医学, 精神科
- **psychologist** 名 心理学者, 精神分析医
- **publication** 名 出版(物), 発行, 発表
- **publish** 動①〜を発表[公表]する ②〜を出版[発行]する
- **pure** 形①純粋な, 混じりけのない ②罪のない, 清い
- **pursue** 動①(〜を) 追う, 〜につきまとう ②〜を追求する, 〜に従事する
- **puzzle** 動〜を迷わせる, 当惑する[させる] 名①難問, 当惑 ②パズル puzzle over 頭を悩ませる, 当惑する

Q

- **quality** 名①質, 性質, 品質 ②特性 ③良質
- **questioner** 名 質問者
- **quotation** 名①引用, 引用文〔句〕 ②相場, 時価 ③見積り

R

- **Rancho de la Cañada** ランチョ・デラ・カニャダ《地名》
- **range** 名 列, 連なり, 範囲 動①並ぶ[並べる] ②〜に及ぶ
- **rapidly** 副 速く, 急速, 素早く, 迅速に
- **rare** 形①まれな, 珍しい, 逸品の ②希薄な ③(肉が) 生焼けの, レアの
- **rate** 名①割合, 率 ②相場, 料金 at any rate とにかく 動①〜を見積もる, 評価する[される] ②〜に等級をつける
- **raw** 形①生の, 未加工の ②未熟な 名 なまもの raw material 資料
- **reader** 名①読者 ②読本, リーダー
- **reality** 名 現実, 実在, 真実(性)
- **realize** 動 〜を理解する, 〜を実現する
- **recent** 形 近頃の, 近代の
- **recognize** 動 〜を認める, 〜を認識[承認]する
- **recollection** 名①思い出, 記憶(力) ②平静
- **recommend** 動①〜を推薦する ②〜を勧告する, 忠告する
- **reconstruction** 名 再建, 復興, 復元
- **reconstructor** 名 再建者, 復興者
- **refer** 動 〜に言及する, 触れる, 〜を参照する
- **reference** 名 言及, 参照, 照会
- **refuse** 動 (〜を) 拒絶する, 断る 名 くず, 廃物
- **regard** 名①注意, 関心 ②尊敬, 好感 ③《-s》(手紙などで) よろしくというあいさつ 動①〜を…と見なす ②〜を尊敬する, 〜に重きを置く ③〜と関係がある with regard to 〜については
- **region** 名①地方, 地域 ②範囲
- **relate** 動 関連がある, 関わる, うまく折り合う
- **relation** 名①(利害) 関係, 間柄 ②親戚 in relation to 〜に関して
- **relationship** 名 関係, 関連, 血縁関係
- **relaxation** 名 息抜き, くつろぎ, 緩和, 弛緩
- **relevant** 形①関連のある, 関連のある ②(今日的) 意味のある ③相当する

A Technique for Producing Ideas

- **remarkable** 形 ①異常な, 例外的な ②注目に値する
- **rentier** 名 金利生活者, 不労所得生活者《フランス語》
- **repeat** 動 (~を)繰り返す 名 繰り返し, 反復, 再演
- **reply** 動 答える, 返事をする, 応答する 名 答え, 返事, 応答
- **reputation** 名 評判, 名声
- **require** 動 ①~を必要とする, ~を要する ②~を命じる, ~を請求する
- **reservoir** 名 貯水池, 貯蔵所, 石油〔ガス〕タンク, (知識などの)蓄積
- **response** 名 応答, 反応, 返答
- **rest on** 熟 ~に基礎をおく, ~を当てにする
- **restless** 形 落ち着かない, 不安な
- **result** 名 結果, 成り行き, 成績 動 (結果として)起こる[生じる], 結局~になる
- **reveal** 動 (隠されていたもの)を明らかにする, 暴露する
- **revolutionize** 動 大変革〔革命〕をもたらす, 根本的に変える
- **rhetoric** 名 レトリック, 修辞(学), 話術
- **Riesman** 名 リースマン《人名》
- **Robert Hutchins** ロバート・ハチンス《人名》
- **romance** 名 恋愛(関係, 感情), 恋愛〔空想, 冒険〕小説
- **Roosevelt** 名 ルーズベルト《人名》
- **routine** 名 お決まりの手順, 日課 形 いつもの, 日常の
- **ruefully** 副 悲しそうに, 残念そうに
- **rule-breaking** 形 規則を破る

S

- **sake** 名 ~のために, ~の目的で, ~に免じて **for one's own sake** 自分自身のために
- **sale** 名 販売, 取引, 大売出し
- **salesmen** 名 salesman(セールスマン)の複数形
- **Sard Harker** 『サード・ハーカー』《小説のタイトル》
- **saying** 名 ①ことわざ, 言い習わし ②言う[言った]こと
- **scan** 動 ~にざっと目を通す, ~を細かく調べる, ~をスキャンする 名 スキャン, 精査
- **scheme** 名 計画, スキーム, たくらみ, 仕組み, 枠組み
- **schoolteacher** 名 学校の教師, 先生
- **scientific** 形 科学の, 科学的な
- **scorn** 名 軽蔑, 冷笑 動 軽蔑する, さげすむ
- **scrapbook** 名 スクラップブック
- **screen** 名 仕切り, 幕
- **search** 動 (~を)捜し求める, 調べる 名 捜査, 探索, 調査
- **seek** 動 捜し求める, 求める
- **seem** 動 ~に見える, ~のように思われる
- **seldom** 副 まれに, めったに~ない
- **self-expanding** 形 自分で成長する, 自己解凍式の
- **selling** 名 販売, セールス
- **semantic** 形 言語意味論, セマンティックス
- **sense** 名 ①感覚 ②《-s》正気, 本性 ③常識, 分別 ④意味 動 ~を感じる
- **separate** 動 分離[分割]する[させる], 別れる[別れさせる] 形 分かれた, 別れた
- **series** 名 一続き, 連続, シリーズ
- **serious** 形 ①まじめな, 真剣な ②重大な, 深刻な, (病気などが)重い
- **shape** 名 ①形, 姿, 型 ②状態, 調子 動 ~を形作る, ~を具体化する

Word List

- **shave** 動(ひげ・顔を)そる, 削る 名ひげそり, 剃髪, 削り(くず)
- **Sherlock Holmes** シャーロック・ホームズ《人名》
- **shift** 動移す, 変える, 転嫁する 名変化, 移動
- **shirk** 動怠ける, 避ける, 責任を逃れる 名責任逃れ, 怠け者
- **shortly** 副まもなく, すぐに
- **shown** 動show(～を見せる)の過去分詞
- **silly** 形愚かな, 思慮のない 名馬鹿者
- **similarity** 名類似(点), 相似
- **similarly** 副同様に, 類似して, 同じように
- **simply** 副①簡単に ②単に, ただ
- **single** 形たった一つの, 独身の 名(ホテルなどの)1人用の部屋, シングルス[単試合]
- **sizable** 形かなり大きい
- **snob** 名俗物, 紳士気取りの人
  snob appeal 俗物根性に訴える要素
- **soap** 名石けん 動(～を)石けんで洗う
- **social** 形①社会の, 社会的な ②社交的な, 愛想のよい
- **sociologist** 名社会学者
- **solution** 名①分解, 溶解 ②解決, 解明, 回答
- **something** 代①ある物, 何か ②いくぶん, 多少
- **sometimes** 副ときどき
- **somewhat** 副いくらか, やや, 多少 代いくぶん
- **sort** 名種類, 品質 動～を分類する
  sort of 多少, いくぶん
- **soul** 名①魂 ②精神, 心
- **source** 名源, 原因, もと
- **southwest** 名形南西(の), 南西部(の)

- **Spanish** 形スペインの 名スペイン語[人]
- **Spanish-American** 名スペイン系アメリカ人
- **spare** 動①～を取っておく ②(～を)惜しむ, 節約する 形暇の, 予備の 名予備品
- **spark** 名①火花 ②ひらめき, 輝き
- **spatially** 副空間的に
- **specific** 形明確な, はっきりした, 具体的な
- **speculate** 動①思索する, 推測する ②投機する speculate on ～ ～に思いを巡らす
- **speculative** 形①思索的な, 思惑の ②投機的な
- **speculator** 名①思索家, 投機家 ②相場師
- **spirit** 名①霊 ②精神, 気力
- **spot** 名①地点, 場所 ②斑点, しみ 動～に点を打つ, ～にしみをつける
- **spouse** 名配偶者
- **staff** 名職員, スタッフ
- **stage** 名①舞台 ②段階 動～を上演する
- **state** 名①有様, 状態 ②《the-》国家, (アメリカなどの)州 動～を述べる 形国家の
- **steady-going** 形着実な, 堅実な
- **stimulate** 動①～を刺激する, 興奮させる ②元気づける
- **stock** 名①貯蔵 ②仕入れ品, 在庫品 ③株式 動仕入れる, 蓄える
- **stockholder** 名株主
- **store away** 熟しまっておく, 蓄える
- **strain** 動①～を緊張させる, ～をぴんと張る ②～を曲解する ③～を無理に曲げる 名①緊張 ②過労, 負担
- **strike** 動①(～を)打つ, ぶつかる ②(災害などが)急に襲う 名①ストライキ ②打つこと, 打撃

A TECHNIQUE FOR PRODUCING IDEAS

- **struck** 動 strike（(～を)打つ, 急に襲う）の過去, 過去分詞
- **stuck** 動 stick（(突き)刺さる[刺す]）の過去, 過去分詞 be [get] stuck 動けなくなる, 行き詰まる
- **submit** 動①服従する, 服従させる ②提出する
- **success** 名 成功, 幸運, 上首尾
- **successful** 形 成功した, うまくいった
- **sudden** 形 突然の, 急な
- **suggest** 動①～を暗示する ②～を提案する
- **suggestion** 名①提案, 忠告, 気配, 暗示
- **supply** 動 ～を供給[配給]する, ～を補充する 名 供給(品), 給与, 補充
- **support** 動①～を支える ②～を養う, ～を援助する 名①支え ②援助, 扶養
- **suppose** 動 ～と仮定する, ～と推測する
- **surely** 副 確かに, きっと
- **surface** 名 表面, 水面
- **suspect** 動（～を)疑う, ～ではないかと思う 名 容疑者, 注意人物
- **suspend** 動 ぶらさがる, つるす, 一時停止する, 延期する 名 一時停止 suspended animation 人事不省, 仮死状態
- **symbol** 名 シンボル, 象徴
- **synthesis** 名 総合, 合成, 統合体
- **systematically** 副 体系的に, 組織的に, 制度的に

T

- **take place** 熟 行われる, 起こる
- **tale** 名①話, 物語 ②うわさ, 悪口
- **technician** 名 技術者, 専門家
- **technique** 名 テクニック, 技術, 手法
- **television** 名 テレビ
- **tend** 動①《– to》～の傾向がある, ～しがちである ②向かう, 行く
- **tentacle** 名 触腕, 触毛,（タコなどの）足, 触覚
- **tentative** 形 仮の, 試験的な 名 仮説, 試案
- **term** 名①期間, 期限 ②語 ③条件
- **text** 名 本文, 原本, テキスト, 教科書
- **theater** 名 劇場
- **theory** 名 理論, 学説, ～論[説] *Theory of the Leisure Class*『有閑階級の理論』
- **thereafter** 副 それ以来, 従って
- **thereby** 副 それによって, それに関して
- **therefore** 副 したがって, それゆえ, その結果
- **thinker** 名 思想家, 考える人
- **Thos, Nelson & Sons** トス, ネルソン＆サンズ《社名》
- **though** 接①～にもかかわらず, ～だが ②たとえ～でも 副 しかし
- **thrill** 名 スリル, 身震い 動 ぞっとする（させる), わくわくする（させる)
- **throughout** 前 ～の至るところに 副 初めから終わりまで
- **thus** 副①このように ②これだけ ③かくて, だから
- **tidy** 形 整然とした, こぎれいな 動 ～を整頓する, ～を処理する
- **tone** 名 音, 音色, 調子 動 調和する[させる]
- **tool** 名 道具, 用具, 工具
- **topic** 名 話題, 見出し
- **trade** 名 取引, 貿易, 商業 動 取引する, 貿易する, 商売する
- **tradition** 名 伝統, 伝説, しきたり
- **transform** 動 変形[変化]する, 変える, 変形[変化]させる

Word List

- **translate** 動 翻訳する, 訳す, 変形する
- **translation** 名 翻訳, 言い換え, 解釈
- **treatment** 名 取り扱い, 待遇
- **tremendously** 副 恐ろしいほどに, 大いに
- **tribute** 名 ①貢ぎ物, ささげ物, 贈り物 ②賛辞, 感謝のことば
- **tried** 動 try (〜しようと試みる) の過去, 過去分詞 形 確実な, あてになる, 信頼できる
- **trite** 形 陳腐な, 古くさい
- **truth** 名 ①真理, 事実, 本当 ②誠実, 忠実さ
- **type** 名 活字, フォント

U

- **unable** 形《be-to》(人が) 〜することができない
- **unaccountability** 名 不可解さ, 奇妙さ
- **unconscious** 形 無意識の, 気絶した
- **unconsciously** 副 無意識に, 知らず知らずに
- **underlie** 動 〜の基礎となる, 下に横たわる
- **undoubtedly** 副 疑う余地のない
- **unimaginative** 形 想像力のない, つまらない
- **university** 名 (総合) 大学
- **unless** 接 もし〜でなければ, 〜しなければ
- **unseen** 形 目に見えない
- **upon** 前 ①《場所・接触》〜 (の上) に ②《日・時》〜に ③《関係・従事》〜に関して, 〜について, 〜して 副 前へ, 続けて
- **usefulness** 名 役に立つこと, 有用性
- **utilize** 動 〜を利用する, 〜を活用する
- **utter** 形 完全な 動 (声・言葉) を発する

V

- **valuable** 形 貴重な, 価値のある, 役に立つ
- **value** 名 価値, 値打ち, 価格 動 〜を評価する, 〜に値をつける
- **Veblen** 名 ヴェブレン《人名》
- **venture** 動 思い切って〜する, 〜を危険にさらす 名 冒険 (的事業), 危険
- **vicarious** 形 身代わりの, 代理の
- **vicariously** 副 身代わりで, 間接的に
- **vividly** 副 生き生きと, 鮮明に
- **vocabulary** 名 ①語彙 ②単語集
- **Volkswagen Beetle** フォルクスワーゲン・ビートル《フォルクスワーゲン社の車名》
- **volume** 名 ①本, 巻, 冊 ②《-s》たくさん, 多量 ③量, 容積

W

- **W. I. B. Beveridge** W. I. B. ビバレッジ《人名》
- **waken** 動 目を覚まさせる, 起こす
- **Watson** 名 ワトソン《人名》
- **weekly** 形 週に1度の, 毎週の 名 週刊誌
- **well-known** 形 よく知られた, 有名な
- **western** 形 ①西の, 西側の ②西洋の
- **whatever** 代 ①〜するものは何で

も ②どんなこと[もの]が〜とも 形 ①どんな〜でも ②《否定文, 疑問文で》少しの〜も, 何らかの

- **whenever** 接①〜するときはいつでも, 〜するたびに ②いつ〜しても 副一体いつ

- **whether** 接〜かどうか, 〜かまたは…, 〜であろうとなかろうと

- **whole** 形全体の, すべての, 完全な, 満〜, 丸〜 名《the -》全体, 全部

- **whom** 代①誰を[に] ②〜するところの人, その人を[に]

- **William Bernbach** ウイリアム・バーンバック《人名》

- **willing** 形 be willing to do 快く〜する, 〜する気がある

- **wing** 名翼, 羽 **winged messenger** ローマ神話のマーキュリー神のこと

- **woke** 動 wake（目がさめる）の過去

- **wonder** 動①不思議に思う, (〜に)驚く ②〜かしら(と思う) 名驚き(の念), 不思議なもの

- **wool** 名羊毛, 毛糸, 織物, ウール **wool gathering** 放心状態, とりとめのない空想

- **word-symbol** 名言語＝シンボル

- **work-a-day** 形忙しい

- **worked-out** 形解決された, 良い結果となった

- **workmanlike** 形職人らしい, 腕ききの

- **worldwide** 形世界的な, 世界中に広まった 副世界中に

- **worthwhile** 形やりがいのある, 価値のある

- **writer** 名書き手, 作家

Y

- **yield** 動①〜を生じる, 産出する ②〜に譲る, 〜に明け渡す

E-CAT

English **C**onversational **A**bility **T**est
国際英語会話能力検定

● E-CATとは…
英語が話せるようになるためのテストです。インターネットベースで、30分であなたの発話力をチェックします。

www.ecatexam.com

iTEP

● iTEP®とは…
世界各国の企業、政府機関、アメリカの大学300校以上が、英語能力判定テストとして採用。オンラインによる90分のテストで文法、リーディング、リスニング、ライティング、スピーキングの5技能をスコア化。iTEP®は、留学、就職、海外赴任などに必要な、世界に通用する英語力を総合的に評価する画期的なテストです。

www.itepexamjapan.com

ラダーシリーズ
A Technique for Producing Ideas
アイデアのつくり方

2005年8月10日　第1刷発行
2025年6月20日　第7刷発行

著　者　ジェームス・ウェブ・ヤング

発行者　賀川　洋

発行所　IBCパブリッシング株式会社
　　　　〒162-0804 東京都新宿区中里町29番3号
　　　　菱秀神楽坂ビル
　　　　Tel. 03-3513-4511　Fax. 03-3513-4512
　　　　www.ibcpub.co.jp

© The McGraw-Hill Companies, Inc. 2003
© IBC Publishing, Inc. 2005

印刷　株式会社シナノパブリッシングプレス
装丁　伊藤　理恵
組版データ　Adobe Garamond Pro Regular

落丁本・乱丁本は、小社宛にお送りください。送料小社負担にてお取り替えいたします。
本書の無断複写（コピー）は著作権法上での例外を除き禁じられています。

Printed in Japan
ISBN978-4-89684-095-7